Successfully Succinct Stage Speaking

50 Tips, Tidbits, and Success Strategies

Dr. Russell J. Zwanka

Other works include

A Marketing Manual for the Millennium

Category Management Principles

Customer Connectivity in Global Brands and Retailers

Requisite Reading for the Renaissance Retailer

Operating in the New Cuba

Food Retail Management Strategic Cases

Would You Shop Here if You Didn't Work Here?

Customers First. Profits Second.

ISBN-13: 978-1974431748

ISBN-10: 1974431746

Special thanks to those who give me the inspiration
to follow my dreams. Pretty sure you know who you
are ☺

About Dr. Z

Dr. Russell J. Zwanka is a Food Marketing Professor at the State University of New York at New Paltz. Dr. Z teaches Category Management, Food Retail Management, Marketing Principles/ Strategy, and Sales Management.

Dr. Z conceptualized and formed the program and curriculum for the Food Marketing Track at the State University of New York at New Paltz. Zwanka is also CEO of Triple Eight Marketing, a retail organization helping food and beverage brands connect and engage around customer lifestyle and orientation.

Zwanka holds a Doctorate in International Business from ISM in Paris, France. He also holds a Masters of Science in Management from Southern Wesleyan University, and a Bachelors of Science in Psychology from the University of South Carolina.

Russell has spoken at various events, including the Carnegie Mellon Social Media Conference, the University of Manitoba Marketing Conference, the Argyle Executive Forum in New York City, the Hospitality Resource Group's Annual Conference, the Hudson Valley Economic Development Corporation's Beer, Wine, and Cider Event, and the New Paltz Chamber Event.

Additionally, he has served on the IGA Retailer Advisory Board, the Consumer Goods Forum Marketing Committee, the Topco Operations Board, the Hudson Valley Community College School of Marketing Advisory Board, the Hudson Valley Economic Development Corporation Food and Beverage Alliance, the National Grocers Association University Coalition, and the Nielsen Retailer Advisory Committee.

Table of Contents

Introduction

Why would anyone want to speak in front of large audiences? Seriously, it's nerve racking, it's something you think about for weeks, it's something where you try to find every excuse not to do it. So, why do it? Why do we put ourselves through this torture?

Well, because it's exhilarating! It helps your business or your brand, it helps you communicate about something in which you have expertise. And, at the end, you feel an enormous sense of accomplishment. You get the applause, you get to engage with the audience both during and after your presentation, you make life-long connections, and you learn something about yourself. You learn that stepping out of your comfort zone is a good thing. Staying in your little box does not develop you as a person. So, get out there and let's get speaking!

First, before we go into the tips and tidbits learned over a career of speaking in front of large audiences, let's talk about mindset. Getting your head on straight is step one in all matters pertaining to public speaking!

Why are we doing this to ourselves? We could just sit back in the back of the audience and critique the person on stage. Much more fun, right? I would suggest, no. Sitting on the sideline watching is for wimps! Get out there and get up on stage. You grow as a person when you do it.

Overall, in this book, I will be covering things that have made me a better speaker in public, and I'm attempting to pay it forward. Think of how much better the world could be if we all knew how to speak clearly, succinctly, and eagerly. Yes, eagerly. You should want to communicate your message. How is anyone going to know you as a person, as an expert, as a leader, if they do not understand your message? Speaking is about communicating your message.

So, here we go, let's get speaking!

Tips, Tidbits, and Success Strategies

1- Attitude

Before we go anywhere, let's get that attitude on straight.

You want to speak in public.

You want to speak in public.

You want to speak in public.

You want to speak in public.

Okay, got that out of the way. Yes, unless you are going to knit blankets for the rest of your life and sell them online only, you will probably be asked to speak in public at some point. Embrace it. Run towards it. Give it a big hug! Your attitude will determine everything when speaking in public. Get that attitude right and everything will fall in place.

In this book, we are going to assume you have embraced the attitude that public speaking is an endeavor towards which you are drawn. It is a place you want to be. You can do this!

2- Choose the topic

Yes, whomever asked you to speak probably should have some insight into your topic, but they do not have final say. Ask them the general topic they would like you to discuss and then you give them the idea and outline of what you are going to discuss.

They came to you and asked because you must be seen as an expert in whatever they would like to hear. If that is not the case, then go ahead and admit it now. Better to say it now, than have your audience let you know later. But, assuming it's the case, then you drive the topic from there on out. Speaking about someone else's topic, using their agenda, using their talking points- you're going to seem disingenuous at best, and like an all-out charlatan at worst. You drive the topic.

3- Be the expert

Yes, it sounds redundant from the last tip, but take it a little further. Starting from this point until you make the presentation, believe you are the expert. The confidence that comes from knowing that you command your topic well enough to be considered a "speaking engagement level" expert is something to be proud of- so be proud of it! And, guess what, when you get up on stage and someone asks you a challenging question- that confidence level will help. But, more on that later.

Also, please understand being the expert means you should have enough expertise in the field to offer both conceptual as well as applied information and action steps for your audience.

4- Study your topic

Wait, we just decided you were the expert, why do you have to study the topic? Because no one knows everything.

From the moment you agree to the speaking engagement, start your research. You already have an idea what you are going to say, but you need more. In fact, you need a ton more! You should have so much updated information you have studied that there is no way anyone in that room could possibly know more than you. Seriously, this is how prepared you need to be.

Gather everything about the topic: trends, history, evolution, experts in the field, etc. Then, add some time to accumulate information from potential audience members, or the people running the conference. The audience is who you are doing this for, not you. Understanding what will help them is paramount to your success.

5- Write it yourself

No matter if you are doing a straight out talk with nothing as slides, or if you are using some sort of enhancement, you write your own presentation. Nothing is worse than the person standing on stage acting like they are reading this information for the first time. You tend to look like a pompous @$$ who is too important and too busy to write your own material. Write it yourself. In the long run, you'll be glad you did.

Think about it, in the long run, you are the expert. You should be the only one qualified to write what you are going to say. Wear that qualification with pride, do your own work. Your audience will see you for the fascinating person that you are.

6- Have someone fix it

Once again, am I contradicting myself? No, not in this case anyway. You wrote the content and put it all together. Your mind will fill any gaps you leave out, and you will not even something is missing (see what I did there?). Someone needs to proof your work for content, grammar, aesthetics, and whether or not you make sense. You can make sense to yourself sometimes, but need a bit more clarity with others.

And, best choice of someone whose help is the best? A person with zero knowledge of your topic. My brothers are civil engineers and professional hydrologists. Do you think I have any idea what they do all day? Nope. We bounce our writing off each other all the time. Who better to read for understanding than someone with no understanding.

7- Write notes

Have a hard copy and write notes all over it. If you are presenting, and have some slides, the slides should have as few words as possible, and your notes should be copious. Read that one again- slides should be simple, and the background behind the slides should be complex. Same if you are solely speaking and have no slides- have what you are going to say, and have a deeper meaning in notes somewhere.

When I present, I have my notes in "Handouts- six slides per page", and I have notes everywhere. I study them in the morning, in the

14

car, before going up. And then, do I bring them up with me? Read the next tip....

8- Do not use notes

Another contradiction? Nope. I said write notes. I did not say use notes. Use your slides or written words, add notes on your hard copy, and study the heck out of all of them. The flow, the words, the segues, the obvious meanings, the hidden meanings, recent examples- but, when you go to present, you will not be using notes.

Notes will screw you up big time. Trust me, notes are bad. Notes are bad. Notes are bad. You lose your spot, you backtrack to see if you forgot anything, you look down to see where you are- all bad habits when trying to connect with your audience. Trust yourself, you don't need them.

9- If you're going to use notes, please return this book

Really, if you're not going to listen....

In all honesty, not having notes in front of you is something that many people would rather die than do. I am here to tell you, you do not need to die. Remember, you are the expert in the room! Even if you only say around 60% of the things you wanted to say, no one will know! If you practiced with someone, they'll know; but it will be your own little secret.

You see, the ability to flow with your ideas while maintaining eye contact with the audience is worth more than a constant reading of your notes. You've got this! You're okay! Just go do it. No crutches! You can walk!

Should I repeat not using notes one more time? Okay, you probably get it by now.

10- Practice

In no way am I saying to "wing it". You'll look like a bumbling idiot. Practice, practice, then practice some more. The more you practice, the more it will look like you are such a natural that you must never need to practice. As Under Armour says, "It's what you do in the dark that makes you shine in the light"!

The best performers look cool as a cucumber, and smooth as a baby's bottom. The paradox is they didn't get there by not sweating the details. They look smooth, calm, and collected because of the blood, sweat, and tears that go into making your performance one to remember. The experts sweat the small stuff, and practice like they've never spoken in public their entire life.

11- Have a confidant

You need real honest feedback every step of the way. This isn't a situation where you want to gloss over actual tips on how to improve. Nobody starts out as a great speaker. It is a honed practice that improves like a fine red wine over time.

Use a friend and work on this skill together. If you have no friends....enlist in a Dale Carnegie course. Seriously, my time in the Dale Carnegie course was life-changing. You never looked forward to attending class, but came out energized and invigorated! Do it, whether or not you have friends.

12- Slides

If you're going to use slides, that is perfectly fine. I am not suggesting you just talk, sometimes a picture or a few key words gets your message across better. You are there to communicate a message to the audience. If one more visual helps, then you should use a visual. Just make it a picture, or a few words- nothing too in-depth. If you must show data, overlay that data with an interpretation. If someone really wants to see the data, they can find you afterwards. Most just want the answer to, "What are you trying to tell me?".

Another thing about slides, know them back and forth. Slides can make a great point or punchline to an action step or even something a bit humorous. When you have those special slides in the presentation, your delivery needs to be as practiced as a comedian. Comedians are funny because they get their timing down to an art form. Communicating effectively requires timing.

13- Numbers

John Legere, CEO of T-Mobile, famously said, "I don't do public math" when testifying in front of Congress. That is sage advice. First, numbers are just kind of difficult to "move around" on stage in front of thousands, when someone asks you a question about them. Know your numbers, be the expert, but this is a situation where that audience member has had time to prepare after seeing your numbers, has probably pulled out a calculator and crunched something, and really wants to show how smart he or she is – at your expense.

Second, numbers tend to bore people. Unless you are at a mechanical engineer's convention, numbers are not received well at all. Summarize what the numbers say, but do not go through the numbers per se. A lesson on linear regression of the variables to show how you came to your brilliant conclusion will fall dead in the center of the room like an anvil on Wile E. Coyote.

Third, one caveat: if you're in a Board Meeting, you're going to have to know numbers and probably do some public math. If you don't like that, then don't take a position that will have you speaking to the Board. That's just life in boardrooms.

14- Percents

Use percents. Yes, I can hear the mathematicians saying numbers are percents, but hear me out. You are here to connect with your audience and you want them to be enthused by your information. If you keep that in mind, then you should always ask yourself how you can communicate your message more clearly.

And, a simple piece of insight- everyone understands percents! Everyone. If the percent is coming from a small base, then acknowledge that fact as you cover the percents. You're not trying to deceive with percents, you're just trying to communicate clearly.

Once again, everyone understands percents! Use them 100% of the time....

15- Make them laugh

Remember as you build your presentation, you need some humor in there somewhere. It can be a purposely misconstrued slide, it can be something relevant to the audience that is self-deprecating (comedians do this the best), it can be whatever you'd like. Just place a few humor breaks in your speaking. People like people that make them laugh.

And, when you've warmed them up with some intermittent humor, they are primed to listen to your message. Hit the hard stuff, and come back with some humor later. You can do this! It'll take some practice.

One caution, though, don't ask a riddle, or really don't ask anything where you need an audience member to respond correctly. Do that, and guess what, the joke's on you. You'll hear crickets, will have to tell your own punchline, and well- just don't do it.

16- Have control over when you speak

If you are a keynote, then you know when you'll be speaking. Not much to change there. Also, if you're good enough to be a keynote speaker, then you can probably handle dishes being picked up, some unruliness, or pretty much anything. You need a pretty decent comfort level to command a keynote presentation.

For the rest of the presentations, try to be first or last. First means you can kick off with a bang, and honestly, enjoy the rest of your day. Going last means you have had time to engage the crowd, watch other speakers, get to know the conference or event, and then you can add some little "local" tidbits into your presentation. Audiences love when you talk about them like you actually cared to get to know them.

The worst time? You guessed it, after lunch. Uggg, food needs to be digested, the body heats up, you get a little sleepy....then the lights go down for a presentation. Snoozeville! If you can't help but take the after lunch spot, then know you're place. You are going to have to swim uphill on this one. You can do it, but plan for it. You need to be Mr. or Mrs. Happy!

17- Get to know the audience

If you are speaking at a conference, then read everything you can about that conference. If you are flying in, try to get in a day early and walk around. First, life really is about the journey. What the heck are you learning by flying in and flying back out immediately? There are cool things out there!

Second, interspersing a few comments about the city, or its traffic, or a specific monument which makes them proud….well, that's gold! It's like saying someone's name. The most important word in anyone's mind is their own name. Saying something about the town or the attendees is like speaking their name.

And, if there is a social event before your engagement, be there. Introduce yourself, let people know why you are there, thank them for inviting you, and take advantage of the opportunity to understand what makes them click. A speaking engagement is about the listener- not the speaker. Remember that little tidbit, and you'll always have the right frame of mind.

18- Relate it to them

There is nothing worse than a person speaking about a topic and then clearly coming up with how it relates to the present audience on the fly. It's like "here's my presentation, and let me add a little about you at the end of every slide". Wrong thing to do- don't do it.

You may start with something like a template, but do not use the same template for every presentation. Remember, someone asked you to present- that is an honor. Treat it like that. The better customized the presentation, the more you'll be asked to either return again next year, or be asked to present at a different event in the future. If it looks like all you can handle is a regurgitation of something you've already presented, you'll be seen as a "One Hit Wonder". Avoid that label at all costs!

19- Solve something

Along the same lines as tip #18, learn what keeps the audience up at night. Do a significant amount of research on the issues in that industry and try to help solve something. Unless you just have a Barry White voice that everyone loves to hear, you were invited to speak because you can help. Well....help them out!

Even go as far as numbering the solutions, or stating that this is where they should take notes. You're there to be part of the solution. Take my advice, this is the part where everyone will sit up and pay attention. Yes, you need to set perspective and why the solutions are what they are, but clearly communicated action steps and solutions are why people attend conferences and meetings.

20- Anticipate the questions

In selling, we like to say you should anticipate the objections. Similar to that, anticipate the questions. This kind of information should bubble up when you are reviewing your presentation with a neutral party. Preferably using someone not intimately familiar with the topic, so they can ask the "layman's" questions.

Then, once that feedback has been handed to you, work it into the presentation- start with, "And let me clarify that a bit". Like anticipating objections, once you throw them out there- you own them. And, once you own them, you get to control the dialogue.

Even go as far as saying, "You may be asking yourself". It goes a long way towards connecting with your audience when you can pause and show that you want your concepts to stick in their head. They appreciate the concern, and will thank you for your openness.

21- What makes you special?

Yes, you are already special, which is why you have been asked to present. But, what makes you special in the sense that you will be the one they talk about as they file out? What makes you special in the sense that you are the one they will remember and discuss on the flight home, or ride home? As in business, asking yourself "what makes me special?" is a great way to incorporate unique differentiators into your speaking.

You talk from the heart, you have better insight than anyone all day, you can do cartwheels on stage....whatever it is, be memorable. And what about your title, your introduction, your insight not provided by anyone else at the conference, and unheard of before today? These are the things that make you special. You've been there, you've solved that, you've been in their shoes. You are special- show it.

22- Play it loud and proud!

I love music as speaking engagements begin. Music can touch your soul, hit your emotions, connect and engage you; so, why don't we hear more music during presentations? People are afraid it won't be "normal"! Life's too short to be normal. Pick your favorite tunes, songs that mean something, choreograph them, and jam them! Go ahead, you have permission! Just say doctor's orders.

You attend sporting events, and music is everywhere. You go shopping and hear music. You go to weddings and funerals and hear music. Music is the great connector in this world. I feel badly for people who just don't "get" music. Could be the greatest invention ever for mankind. Play it loud!

23- Envision everything

If you can visit the room ahead of time, do it. Make a point of meeting the audiovisual person and talk about how everything is going to run, pick your spots on the stage. Envision a successful presentation. Envision the crowd jumping out of their seats, and crowding around you afterwards just to talk! You have to call security because they all want to talk to you! You're the Beatles!

You could picture it, couldn't you? Well, why wouldn't you plan for every single presentation to knock their socks off? "I'm planning to be

26

mediocre" is not a chant that will help you take the hill. Come on!

In your mind, run through the intro, the magnet to get them drawn into your set, the walking from one spot to the other, the smiles, the transition between slides, the humor. Picture it all. Your mind has a unique way of making your vision into reality.

24- Be the most passionate person in the room

Okay, somebody asked you to speak. They said you're an expert and you can help the audience solve something. They said they wanted to hear you. Get. Excited.

Don't jump all over the stage like a clown, but be to the point where every single person in the audience puts their phones down, stops glancing around, and is sad when you're done. Absolutely sad it had to end. Those with the most passion are highly contagious- in a good way. Be the "burning sun" of your idea or topic. If you're not excited, how can you ask other people to be?

And, similar to not taking my advice on using notes- if you're not able to get "up" for the presentation and be excited as heck about your topic, why are you there? Seriously, why are you wasting your time and their time? It's okay, just don't take the opportunity to speak publicly. Sit there in a corner drooling. Knit afghans.

25- Breathe

Probably the most important lesson of the book. Breathe! Call it a cleansing breath, calling it a calming technique, call it Lamaze, call it whatever; but breathe. Breathe in for maybe five to eight seconds, hold it a second, and breathe out slowly. Takes your heart rate down, clears your mind, and you're ready to go.

Remember, being a little uptight is good. It means you are excited to share your information. If you weren't uptight, you wouldn't be normal. The best speakers, though, know how to channel it into an awesome presentation. That's going to be you! Breathe the entire day, and especially while you are being introduced- the best time to take a nice deep breath and hit the stage!

Now, a little tidbit- unless you are some incredibly fit marathoner, don't run onto the stage. Walk briskly and with energy, but don't run. I've seen it once before, where the speaker ran on stage to show how full or energy he was. Unfortunately for him, and for the rest of us, he ran totally out of breath before speaking- then couldn't catch his breath because....because he had to speak. Just a bad situation. Avoid the situation where you have to catch your breath.

26- Podiums are evil

No, the podium never did anything bad, except gave you shelter- a wall between yourself and those you are trying to reach. You can't reach through a wall. Unless you are the President of a country and could use the extra protection of a podium, get away from it. Get away from it now! It's a crutch, it holds notes (we're not using notes, are we?), it gives you something upon which to rest your hands like you are presiding over a high school awards ceremony. Unless you had a kid winning something grand, has an award ceremony ever left you wanting it to last longer?

If you can, before you speak, have them remove the podium. If not, that's okay, just avoid it. Shake your introducer's hand and pick a spot on the stage. Go to that spot!

27- Use a lapel microphone

Surprisingly, many places do not have any plans to use lanyard, lavalier, or clip-on microphones unless you ask for one. You are to avoid holding a microphone in one hand at all costs. It is like speaking with a hand tied behind your back. We express with both hands. We make gestures with both hands. Measure the appropriate place for the clip ahead of time- where you have maximum amplification and are hands-free.

Speaking of microphone placement, make sure someone professional places it on you and lets you know how to turn it on (better if they control it from the side, if that is possible). Do not place the microphone where you are going to constantly be either looking the wrong direction or will be hitting it with your tie or jacket or beard (it's possible). The strange thing is, when these things happen, usually the speaker is the only one who doesn't realize it. Have a professional clip on the clip on.

And, now that your hands are free, use them! Use them vigorously! We communicate so much through hand gestures, it makes perfect sense to use them effectively as a tool for cementing your message.

28- Who is controlling the slides?

If you are using slides, and I would suggest you have at least some slides, make sure you either control the slide advances or have someone do it who is in tune with your total presentation. Nothing is worse than a speaker having to say, "Please go back". That is not a professionally presented speech, and clearly not successfully succinct stage speaking.

If you are controlling the slides, you will now have a clicker. It will be in your hand. It had better be in your hand....do not have your speech set up so you have to go back to a laptop each time you want to advance to the next slide. Either have a clicker or have a friend. By the way, check the batteries of the clicker before you begin.

29- No lasers!

If you do have a clicker, then you might want to familiarize yourself with the advancing buttons. Don't wait until you want to move your first slide to act like you've never seen a clicker before- go ahead, admit it, we've all been in at least one presentation where the speaker has to say, "How does this work?". Uggg!

And, once you are familiar with it, repeat after me- no laser pointer! Every clicker has a laser pointer. Don't use it. If your slides are so convoluted you need to use a laser pointer, then clean up your slides. You're addressing the symptom, not the problem.

And, if you just don't like listening to me (not sure why you are reading the book), and you go to use a laser pointer- what does everybody notice? What you are trying to point out? Nope, not at all. They are watching to see if your hands are shaking. Everyone in the room knows it can be a terrifying experience to speak in front of a crowd, and for some reason, it validates them to see the speaker's hands shaking.

30- Talk Walk Talk Walk

You've picked your spot on stage (remember that tip?), and you are commanding your room. Now what? Use that stage wisely. Stand still as you are making your point. Move as you are shifting to another point. Moving across the stage should be effortless, smooth, and should be part of the presentation. Don't just move around for the heck of it. Move around to make points, move around to include areas of the room that normally do not feel included, move around to show that this is your room, your stage, your presentation.

And when you want to make the best point of the day, stop! Just stop! Use that time to look around from a stationary position. No distractions, you are making your top point of the day.

32

Pick some people out in each quadrant of the room. Pick those giving you positive non-verbal feedback. They are the ones taking pictures of your slides, nodding positively, sitting up in their chairs, etc. We all need reinforcement once in a while, and picking those providing it makes everything run smoother.

31- Pauses are epic

A pause is not there because you forgot what you were trying to say. The pause is there because you want them to remember what you are saying. Pauses are impactful, so must be used sparingly and balanced. A pause gives weight and importance to the point just made. Plan your pauses. You'll look like a genius.

Go back and think of all the times a speaker has connected with you emotionally. Think of the message and how it was delivered. Was there a pause? I would bet there was some sort of change-up in flow or sentence structure to get you to think. Practice pausing, this is one of those techniques that only the most skilled presenters use well. You can do this!

32- Repeat Repeat Repeat Repeat Repeat

Goes hand in hand with the pause. When you have something impactful to say, a point that should be remembered, plan your pause, stop during your pause and make eye contact with the audience, and then repeat what you just said. Magic! Say your point, make your pause, establish some eye contact, repeat yourself. If you wish, you can even say, "Let me repeat myself." Solid gold!

When you repeat your point, this time with a little more emphasis, it sticks. Look around, make more eye contact than usual. In the annals of speaking tips, this one is right near the top. The pause and the repeat, used effectively, are pretty awesome. Give it a try.

33- Look 'em in the eye!

This is your audience. They are here to listen to you. They are hopefully sitting in rapt attention. Look at them! Look at as many eyes as you can, especially when you want to make a point. When you are making a point, look at a few people, hold the locked eyes for a few seconds, look at some more people. Looking deeply into someone's eyes is like looking deeply into everyone's eyes. They all see what you are doing. They all see you are trying to connect with them. They appreciate it. Eye contact should be embraced. You have nothing to hide! Find someone that makes you happy. Sometimes our default facial expression is neutral or a frown. Practice smiling, even as your default position. If you can find someone in the audience that makes you smile, go back to that face repeatedly. A crowd wants to see someone comfortable enough with his or herself to stand up there and smile.

34- Gesture, Jester

Okay, so you're not trying to be funny the entire time- "gesture" and "jester" just seemed to fit well together. You have no microphone in your hand, you have no podium upon which to rest your weary arms- it's just you and the audience. What are you going to do with your hands? This is a biggie. Your hands can tell your story for you. The wide open arms with the palms to the audience means you are trying to connect. That would be preferred. When you are making a point, use your hands and arms. If asking them something, point to them (in a friendly manner). "What would you do?" with a soft point towards the audience means you'll connect verbally and non-verbally.

A non-verbal embrace of the audience is powerful. Almost like one big group hug. Try it on your next audience, and watch how they emanate towards you. People like gestures, as long as you have a goal and use them to communicate effectively.

35- It's what you're not saying that says so much

Hand in hand (get it?) with the last tip, your non-verbals are communicating over 60% of your message! Stand with your arms wide open in front of a mirror, loosen your neck, stand up straight....pretty much everything Mom would say....it's all true. Be in command up there with both words and body language.

And should we talk about what you should not do? Have to. A good lesson in life, as well as presenting- never fold your arms in front of you. Never! Never! Probably the most off-putting, defensive, closed-in pose ever invented. You might think you're looking pensive and intelligent as you stand there with your arms crossed- you don't. You look like you are defending yourself, like you are just waiting for the shoe to drop.

And, the next one? Of course- hands in your pockets. Pockets are never to be used on stage unless you are a magician. Keep the hands out, keep them moving, use them to communicate. Last one, especially if taking part in a panel discussion? The hands behind the head and/or the legs crossed. Pretty much anything that can be felt by your audience as a defensive (or obnoxious) sign should be avoided. Even kids understand a line through something means "no".

I cannot stress any stronger the power of non-verbals. People ask questions, acknowledge and move towards them. People clap, hold your hands together like a "thank you". People are listening intently, move around confidently and proudly. Think of how a cat walks. Is there any doubt who rules this planet when a cat walks by? No doubt at all. We all serve the cats....

36- Louder!

You are in command up there! Speak like a Broadway actor. Did you ever notice that every time they speak, you hear them all the way at the back of the theatre? Even sometimes without a microphone. It's part of their training. They want their message to get across to every person in the auditorium. They also want to ensure all eyes are on them. How do you do that? You speak like you mean it. Your speaking volume speaks, well....volumes....for your message. You want to be an expert, then sound like an expert.

If you naturally have a soft voice, that's okay. Practice projecting your voice to the back of the room. You can do it. You don't need a baritone to be successful, just be cognizant of the necessity to project your voice.

One more little tip, trying to control your voice downward, while also fighting off butterflies, is not going to work. Your voice will be wavy at best and downright wimpy, at most. And if you don't naturally have a commanding and powerful voice, then fake it till you make it. There is no way around this one. Did you hear me!?!?!?

37- In tone nation

Once you've got the domination volume down pat, then you need to be introduced to intonation, or the rise and fall of your voice. Yelling or being boisterous all the time will only mean "all my points are important". And, if that is your message, then guess what? None of your points will be important.

Just like "let me say this again", you need a way to bring people into your huddle, so to speak. And the best way is to get louder, right? Wrong! Go the opposite direction. Get calmer and a bit softer. Don't whisper, just get softer. The softest words are the ones we hear the best. Try it.

And, when you bring them in, and now want to return to normal- bring them back out. Increase your volume and go forward! Using voice volumes is powerfully effective.

38- Thanky thanky

You were invited into their house to help them with something. That is an honor and a privilege. In fact, tell them it's an honor and a privilege to be here. It seriously should be. A little prep before thanking the audience and hosts: make sure you know of any dignitaries and memorize or write them down, know of any senior members and acknowledge them, if there were sponsors specifically for your speaking event (and they were not already mentioned)- then mention them.

You are to come across as the most gracious and thankful speaker they have ever had. You know why? Because you really should be happy and grateful they chose you to come into their house.

If you do not feel grateful for the opportunity to speak to the group, then once again, turn down the speaking engagement. In this book, we are embracing the opportunity to get our message out there. Be grateful someone cares what you have to say.

39- Start with a bang

That group of highly attentive audience members gives you about 90 seconds to convince them they should listen. Plus, they just heard quite a few accolades from your introducer, so they have set the bar pretty high for you. Start with a bang, start with something funny (keep in mind the humor tips) or something unique to the group or location. You have got to start strong! The group has texts to answer and cats to look at on Instagram.

And, once you start, don't go downhill from there. Prove that listening to you is the correct choice. Remember, these steps: wake them up and start with a bang, tell them what you are going to cover, cover it, and tell them what you just covered.

40- Where's the cred?

In just a few sentences, and only if your introducer did not cover it, you need to quickly establish credibility with the audience. They probably think you're the best person to be speaking at the time, but now is the time to complete re-affirm that assertion. You can mention your career length, your companies, your number of books, some successes, etc. It's not Boasting Hour, but you do need to let them know you belong on that stage.

Plus, as you speak, a few "this is what we did in this situation" additions go a long way. You are not new to this business or this topic. If you were, you wouldn't be asked to speak. Show that you belong on stage.

41- Dress the part

Yes, it might be a developer's conference, or an engineering conference- places where a tie would be seen as an affront to the audience. But, barring any major issues with ties or a really nice outfit, you should aim to be the best dressed person in the room. Why not? You're being asked to deliver a message and come across as an expert. Nothing says "expert" more than looking the part.

As a lesson in life, how about dress each day like you're going to meet the Queen of England. Think of the British royalty. Look at them. Okay, we have really no idea what the various princes and princesses actually do, but we do unequivocally know they are some serious dressers. They look great! What's wrong with that? You always know who is royalty, right? Why not make it obvious who's in charge?

Once again, as in life, looking good makes you feel good. I know how Mark Zuckerberg dresses. That's okay, for him. You will not be able to pull off the "hoodie and jeans" look for long. Zuckerberg doesn't care.

42- Be the expert

If you are not the expert, then what are you doing on stage? If there are certain areas you are not as well-versed as others, then get up to speed. Any hesitation when questions are being asked, and it's all over. You have lost the room. You should prepare so well, you could give a class on the topic. If anyone really wanted every single data point and scenario on the topic, you could do that. At that point, you've earned the right to stand on that stage.

I understand it seems like I've repeated this one a couple of times. It's because I have. Being the expert is one of the most singularly important aspects of public speaking. The power could go out, and your slides could spontaneously combust- and you could stand up there and just keep going. That's what an expert looks like.

43- What's the frequency, Kenneth?

Are you speaking to random people who attended because it was a nice day out of the office? Or, are you speaking to a group of experts, and it's a sharing conference on the latest insights and expertise developments. Clearly, the level of expertise in the room should be determined ahead of time- and your presentation should be tailored towards that level of knowledge. Come in too low, and they immediately pull out the phones. Come in too high, and....they immediately pull out the phones. Granted, some people are going to pull out their phones either way, but you don't have to give them a reason.

If you are having trouble gauging the expertise level, or it is too varied for one genre of presentation, then get there early and ask around. See what is one their minds as you socialize. It will tell you a ton about how much they know on your subject.

44- What if the power went out?

Are you prepared to give your talk even if all props, all assistance, all lighting, everything went blank? If so, then go for it. If not, and you are depending upon crutches to help guide you where you're going, then it is suggested you double back and learn your material. Think of teaching a class and someone asks a solid and detailed question that de-rails your notes for the day- are you confident enough in your ability to just go with it?

Yes, I have said it before. Stand in the dark and go through your presentation. When you get to the point where you could give your presentation without notes or slides, then think about how much more powerful it'll be when you add back in the slides.

45- You need a story

What is it about you that makes you interesting? I would suggest the opener be a story. We all love stories. So tell one. You started as a poor sharecropper's kid and rose to CEO. You have always been shy, but now speak in front of thousands. Make the story something personal and maybe even a bit disarming. You're not a big full-of-yourself speaker, you're a human who wants to help. You're a person just like the audience. That's a story worth hearing.

And when your story is done, relate it to the topic. You started as a bagger in a grocery store working for tips at 12 years old, and then rose to run merchandising and marketing in multiple organizations? You only worked in the industry

44

until you could find a "real job", but stuck with it because you liked it? Those are real stories worth telling. They are credibility builders.

46- Disarm them

Show how you can relate. You used to sit there and wonder how you could ever speak to a group. And then, you went to Dale Carnegie classes and love speaking to a large audience! You are secretly introverted to a fault, but can fake it in front of a group. See how these things relate to the audience? They make you seem genuine. It primes them to listen to you. Because, after all, you're just like them.

We see politicians take off their ties and roll up their sleeves when they are campaigning. It's about connecting with the listener. Looking like an everyday person works sometimes. Looking like the best dressed person in the room also works sometimes. Know what connects. Disarming the audience primes them to connect with you.

47- Emotion connects

When telling your story, tell it from the heart, and tell something that makes you choke up. You don't have to choke up every time, and you certainly should not fake it like a politician; but tell something that any emotional human being will see as deeply touching and heartfelt. Emotion "primes the pump" to enjoying what you're about to hear. Remember, you want to be remembered. Remember? When they leave, you've touched them in their heart. That's a great speech!

In advertising, we hear the piano and know that something emotional is on its way. That's how I want you to deliver your message. Picture yourself talking one on one to your best friend. That type of genuine speaking is the gold standard. All the best use emotion in their delivery.

48- Call an audible

The audience is not always going to be primed to listen. It might be right after lunch, the last speaker might have bored them to tears, the overall event might be winding down. Whatever it is, the audience may not always respond the way you'd like them to respond. That's perfectly fine. You're ready for this!

Have some way to shift gears, to vector, in another direction. Whether it's simply changing the subject, or having a funny story to get them back on your page- have it in your back pocket.

There will be times when the audience is dead and needs motivation- it's like a Friday morning 8:00AM class in college. It takes a special professor to teach Friday mornings at 8:00AM!

Diverting from your plan based upon your observations is perfectly fine. We've all sat there as someone droned on while the entire crowd has mentally left the building. Don't be that person. You are already looking at the audience. Work to understand their level of engagement and go with it. You'll be glad you did.

49- Be compelled to action

You're there to help. Similar to the point on saying when to take notes, be specific about action steps, and immediate things people in the audience can do *right now* to improve their business.

Being action-oriented is a good lesson in life as well. Theory is great. But, unless you can apply that theory, you're useless to the audience. Understand they need to go back to work and show that attending the conference was worth time away from the desk. Give them something to work with!

50- You You You

You are talking to the audience. Make it about them. "**You** can take these steps and implement", "**You** can address this situation tomorrow morning", etc. It's about them, not about your expertise and how the speaker acts. It's how you want the audience to act.

Similar to hearing your own name, hearing how they can incorporate what you are saying is magical and golden to any audience member. Think of the audience first.

Conclusion

So, there you have it. Fifty quick and easy tips, tidbits, hints, and effectiveness tools to be used in making all of us better public speakers. In fact, it'll make us **Successfully Succinct Stage Speakers**!

The game is on! Step up to the three-point line and shoot! The worse thing that can happen is you miss. And, is that really a bad thing? Plus, you've read this book and are trying to improve. I would bet you're going to hit that three-pointer.

The game of life is here and now, go for it!

~ Dr. Z

Made in the USA
Lexington, KY
25 November 2017